MAGIC TRICKS
for Children

Magic box

BARRON'S

New York · Toronto

First edition for the United States and Canada published
1989 by Barron's Educational Series, Inc.

First published in the UK 1989 by
Crocodile Books Ltd.

All inquiries should be addressed to :
Barron's Educational Series, Inc.
250 Wireless Boulevard
Hauppauge, New York 11788

Library of Congress Catalog Card No. 89-6509

International Standard Book No. 0-8120-4289-1

Library of Congress Cataloging-in-Publication Data

Collis, Len.
   Magic tricks for children / by Len Collis; illustrated by
Eira Reeves.
        p.   cm.
   Summary: Presents routines for young magicians, featuring simple tricks,
stories, and jokes.
   ISBN 0-8120-4289-1
   1. Tricks--Juvenile literature.   (1. Magic tricks.)
I. Reeves, Eira, ill.   II. Title.
GV1548.C64   1989
793. 8--dc19   89-6509
9012   98765432   CIP
Printed in Italy   AC

Introduction

Magic isn't what it used to be, thank goodness!

When I was very young, I remember spending hour after patient hour practicing tricks with coins, cards, rings, handkerchiefs and countless small objects tucked up my sleeve (which either stuck there and wouldn't come down or kept falling out all the time).

To perform just one measly trick well seemed to require months of painstaking rehearsal and dedication. Props were cumbersome, conjuring was a skill to be learned, and there were no short cuts.

You'll be pleased to know that the tricks in this book aren't like that at all. Magic has changed, and what people expect of a magician has changed, too.

Baffling your audience and impressing them with hard-won skills is no longer what's required (if it ever was). Today's magicians are entertainers, and everything is much more fun.

Most of the tricks in this book will take you only a minute or two to master. Some are so simple that they won't even take that long. They have all been chosen because they are fun to see done and just as much fun to perform.

Many of them are woven around stories or jokes. The emphasis is on the "routine" rather than the magic.

All of which makes this book of tricks rather different from others you may have seen. I hope you enjoy reading it as much as I have enjoyed writing it.

Len Collis

Warning

Part of the fun of being a magician is in making the props and equipment you want to use, so this book explains how to do just that. But if you are not old enough to handle some of the tools required, like pins and scissors, then get a grown-up or an elder brother or sister to help.

Remember: tools with cutting edges and sharp points are DANGEROUS if not used properly. Similarly, when you are performing tricks that involve any of these dangerous items, be careful. If you can afford to buy these items do make sure you get the safety type— round-ended scissors, safety pins, plastic knives. The golden rule is: Better safe than sorry.

Contents

Making your props

Make a magic wand

You will need:

12 inches (30cm) of round wooden dowel rod,
   about a ¼ inch (1cm) in diameter

a sheet of fine sandpaper

black glossy paint

white glossy paint

masking or transparent tape

A wand is something every magician has, so you shouldn't be without one!

Lumber yards and many hardware stores all stock wooden dowel in various lengths and thicknesses.

Sandpaper the ends of the rod to make them nicely rounded, then paint them white, covering about 2 inches (5cm) of the dowel at each end. Use two or three coats of your white paint to get a good finish, allowing each coat to dry before putting on the next coat.

When the white paint is dry and hard, wrap a strip of masking or transparent tape around the white paintwork at the spot where it joins the bare wood at each end of the rod. Now paint the middle of the rod with black paint. Add two

COVER THE ENDS OF THE ROD WITH TAPE...

...THEN PAINT THE MIDDLE SECTION BLACK.

more coats of paint and wait for it to dry. The tape will prevent the black paint from running into the white areas and give you a perfect edge.

ABRACADABRA!

Peel off the tape, and your wand is now ready for use.

Make a magic spell book

You will need:

an old storybook or other hardcover book you don't need any more

a sheet of colored construction paper (red is best)

some aluminum foil

glue

a felt-tip black pen

scissors

tracing paper

pencil

transparent tape

No, witches aren't the only ones who keep books of magic spells! Magicians need them too.

Your spell book, alas, won't have any spells in it. It will simply be an old storybook dressed up to look the part. But nobody in the audience needs to know that!

Start by cutting the construction paper to the right size for covering the outside of the book. You can do this by opening the book somewhere in the middle, laying it on the sheet of paper, and measuring off a slightly larger area all around. You should allow about an inch extra (3cm) at the top and bottom, and one-and-a-half inches (4cm) at the sides. Now cut and fold the paper around the book as our drawing shows, and fasten the inside edges with transparent tape.

MEASURE AND CUT THE PAPER AROUND THE BOOK.

THEN FOLD AND STICK THE PAPER DOWN AS NEATLY AS YOU CAN.

Write MAGIC SPELL BOOK in bold letters on the front cover and along the spine, then cut stars, half-moons, and other spooky shapes you want from the aluminum foil, and glue them to the front and back. Make sure you leave enough room to include the black cat in our drawing. Trace the outline onto the front cover, then color it in with the black felt-tip pen.

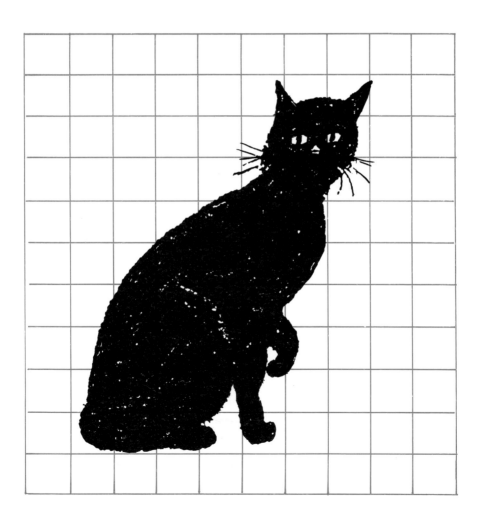

Magic for friends and parties

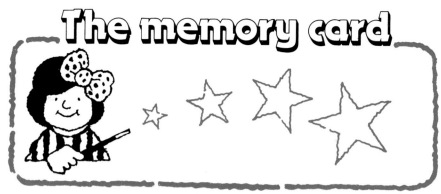

The memory card

You will need:

a deck of cards

This is a neat little trick and requires no magic skill whatsoever.

Take any fifteen cards from the deck and deal them face upwards in three piles of five cards each. Ask a friend to look at the cards as you deal them, remember one particular card, and tell you which pile it's in.

Gather up the cards and repeat the process twice. Then hold the last pile selected behind your back and ask your friend to think hard about the chosen card.

Hey, presto, from behind your back you produce the exact card your friend had in mind!

THE SECRET: When you gather up the cards after each deal, make sure the pile with the chosen card in it is BETWEEN the other two piles.

Then, after the third deal, the chosen card will always be the MIDDLE one in the pile.

That means it is the THIRD card (from either end), and it is easy to find when the cards are held behind your back.

IMPORTANT: When you deal the cards, put one card in the first pile, one in the second, and one in the third. Then go back and put a second card in the first pile, a second card in the second pile, and a second card in the third pile. Continue in this way until all 15 cards are dealt. *Do not* deal five consecutive cards in the first pile, then five in the second, and five in the third. The trick won't work if you deal this way.

Two little blackbirds

You will need:

two small stickers or squares of gummed paper

Toddlers and very small children love this simple trick and never seem to spot how it's done.

You stick one of the squares on the middle fingernail of your left hand, and the other on the middle fingernail of your right hand. (The glue of press-on note stickers isn't strong enough to stay in place during this trick.)

Then you tap the two fingers on a tabletop and chant:

Two little blackbirds
Sitting on a wall
One named Peter
One named Paul.
Fly away Peter
Fly away Paul
Come back Peter
Come back Paul.

On the words "Fly away...," the gummed squares disappear one at a time. When you say "Come back...," they reappear again!

THE SECRET: You substitute the middle fingers with two others to make Peter and Paul "disappear," then reverse the procedure to bring them back again!

It works like this: keep your hands bunched during the rhyme with just each middle finger extended. The other fingers are tucked into your palms and out of sight below the level of the table.

On the words "Fly away Peter," raise your left hand sharply into the air, bringing the middle finger into your palm at the same time.

Then drop your hand down to the table again, but this time with your first finger (NOT the middle one) stuck out.

Do the same with your right hand on the words "Fly away Paul." Then reverse the movements when you say "Come back Peter, Come back Paul."

"ONE NAMED PETER..."   "... ONE NAMED PAUL"

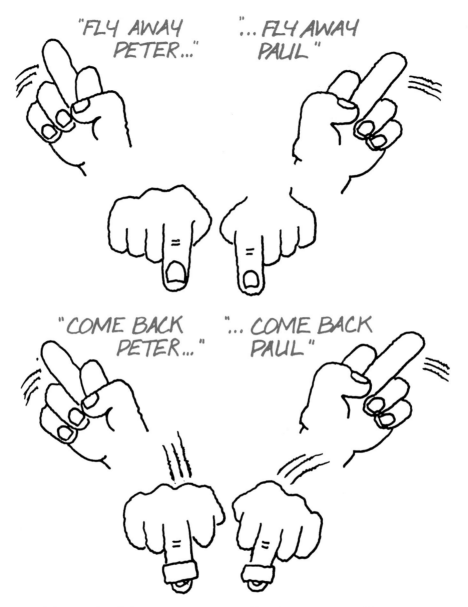

Now do I hear you say that every self-respecting four-year-old would spot how a trick like THAT was done?

Try it and see. They don't, they just don't!

The swinging bottle

You will need:

an empty bottle of dishwashing detergent

a thick shoelace

the cork from a wine bottle

a penknife

sandpaper

This trick is big enough to include in a stage show, but you can also perform it in close-up company without anyone spotting how it's done.

Take an ordinary empty plastic container—the sort that holds dishwashing detergent is ideal—and show it to the audience.

SHOW THE EMPTY BOTTLE TO THE AUDIENCE.

Then hold up a thick shoelace, or a piece of thick string 12 inches (30cm) long.

Very carefully, thread the end of the lace into the bottle. Now tip the bottle over.

Of course, the lace should fall back out. But it doesn't.

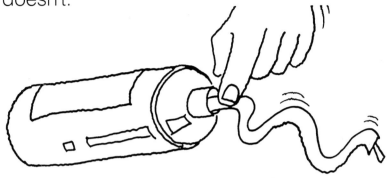

NOW THREAD THE LACE INTO THE BOTTLE.

Magically, it has become so firmly fixed inside that you can take the other end of the lace and swing the bottle back and forth. Incredible!

WHEN YOU TIP THE BOTTLE UP... THE LACE STAYS INSIDE!

THE SECRET: A little cork ball, concealed in the palm of your hand, has been slipped inside the container BEFORE the lace is put in. When the bottle is tipped upside down, the cork drops to the neck of the container and jams against the lace so that neither will come out.

PREPARATION: Cut the wine-bottle cork roughly to size with your penknife. Then whittle around the edges to form it into the shape of a ball. Don't trim away too much—the cork should be just small enough to pass through the neck of the bottle without binding, and that's all. Use the sandpaper to smooth off any lumpy parts or bulges.

YOU MUST BE **VERY CAREFUL** WHEN YOU ARE USING THE KNIFE! GET A GROWN-UP To HELP!

When it's exactly the right size, practice concealing it in your palm and easing it unnoticed into the container. The best moment to do this is when the shoelace is held up to the audience, and their attention is distracted away from the bottle.

The baffling balloon

You will need:

a red balloon

a blue balloon

a pencil

a safety pin

This is a super trick to start off your magic show.

You hold up a large red balloon. Then you take a safety pin and wave it threateningly at the balloon. Of course your audience realizes exactly what you intend to do next! And they're right—you plunge the safety pin straight into the balloon.

But instead of bursting, it turns into a blue balloon!

THE SECRET: The blue balloon is INSIDE the red one, but not blown up so much. When the safety pin bursts the red balloon, the blue one inside is left unharmed—and it looks as if the red balloon has magically changed color.

PREPARATION: Before the balloons are blown up, the blue one must be pushed inside the red one. Use the blunt end of a pencil to do this, and leave a little of the blue end sticking out.

Now carefully blow up the blue balloon to a reasonable size and tie a knot in the end. The red balloon, which is on the outside, will naturally inflate as well, but you will need to blow it up a little more so that it is about one inch (2cm) larger than the blue balloon.

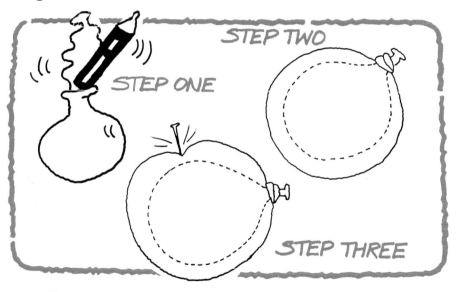

Remember, there must be enough space between the two balloons for you to be able to burst the outer one without damaging the one inside.

When you've blown up the red balloon so that it is well clear of the blue one, tie a knot in the end, and you will be ready to start.

Chicken thieves

You will need:

nine small candies (not sticky ones), all the same color

This isn't really a trick at all, but small children still find it baffling.

Start by placing seven of the candies in a row in the middle of the table. Put the other two candies in front of you. Then tell this story:

"This is the tale of two thieves (pick up the two candies in front of you, one in each hand) who set out to steal some chickens.

"They crept into the chicken farm with their sacks and took all the chickens they could find." (Pick up one of the seven candies in the middle of the table in your RIGHT hand, the next in your left hand and so on alternately until all the candies in the middle have been gathered up.)

"But suddenly the farmer came rushing out so they had to put them all back." (Replace the seven candies, one at a time, in the middle of the table, starting with one from your LEFT hand. Then lay one from your right hand and continue alternately as before. But make sure you keep your hands closed all the time. When the seven candies are returned, the audience will believe you have a candy in each hand as before. In fact, both are now in your RIGHT hand.)

BOTH "CHICKENS" ARE NOW IN YOUR **RIGHT HAND!**

"They hid until the farmer had gone away, and then crept back and stole them again." (As before, pick up seven candies, one at a time alternately, starting with your RIGHT hand.)

"Then they ran off as fast as they could. But before they had gone very far they began to quarrel and fight over who should have the most chickens.

"This thief (put down a candy from your left hand) lost the fight and finished up with only two chickens." (Open your left hand and show there are only two candies there.)

"But THIS thief (put down a candy from your right hand) won the fight and took home FIVE chickens." (Now open your right hand and show five candies.)

Simple, isn't it? But you'll be amazed how often the audience will think they've been fooled by your incredible sleight of hand!

Simon says

You will need

six used matches (you *must* make sure they are dead ones)

a drinking straw

a bowl of water

a little soap and sugar

Here's a baffling illusion that you can perform in very close company.

First, float six matches in the bowl of water. Then dip the straw into the middle and say: "Simon says go back." Sure enough, all the matches immediately start drifting out toward the edge of the bowl!

Now you take out the straw, wave it over the bowl like a wand, and say: "Simon says come close." You dip the straw back into the water

and, hey presto, the matches start floating in toward the middle!

THE SECRET: The straw must be carefully "treated" before you start. Fill one end with soap, and dip the other end in moist sugar. Then wipe the tips clean so that nobody can see what you've done.

When you dip the soaped end into the water, the matches will move outward. When the other end goes in, the sugar makes them come back to the middle.

Waving the straw like a wand over the bowl gives you the chance to "switch ends" without arousing suspicion!

Match play-1

You will need:

a matchbox

six used matches

a crayon

your book of magic spells

This trick can be performed on its own but it's much more fun to combine it with the trick on the next page.

On the table in front of you is a half-open matchbox and a crayon. You tell the audience you would like someone to take a used match, any match, from the box and mark it with the crayon for identification.

But when you pick up the matchbox and glance inside, there is a problem—it's empty!

Clearly you have forgotten to check that there were matches in it before starting the trick!

You turn the box upside down and shake it in the forlorn hope that an odd match might fall out but nothing does.

"Perhaps we'll do something else instead,"

you mutter, shutting the box and putting it back on the table.

Then an idea strikes you. A magic spell might get you out of trouble!

You pick up the spell book and leaf through it quickly. You find the right page and say: "Obbligobblidubbli and...and," peering closely at the words, "inkitwinki...no, inkiwinki...no, twinki...oh, this is hopeless, I can't even pronounce it!"

You throw down the book in disgust, and pick up the matchbox to put away. But as you do so, it rattles!

You open it in disbelief and find six matches inside. The spell must have worked even though you couldn't say it properly!

THE SECRET: The matches were in the box all the time, of course. They were wedged between the open tray and the roof of the box.

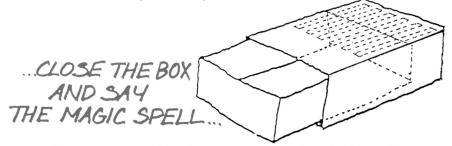

...CLOSE THE BOX
AND SAY
THE MAGIC SPELL...

As soon as the box was pushed shut the matches became unwedged and fell down into the tray.

Now go on to the next trick...

You will need:

a good quality white handkerchief with a hem

the crayon from the previous trick

the matchbox and matches from the previous trick

a spare match

You invite a member of the audience to take a match out of the matchbox and put a crayon mark on it for identification.

Then open out the handkerchief to show there is nothing concealed in it, and wrap it around the match.

When the handkerchief is folded up, you tell the audience that you know the match is still inside because you can feel it through the folds.

To prove it, you let someone in the audience feel it, too. When they are satisfied that the match is there, tell them to snap it in half. They do this, through the handkerchief, and make sure it is thoroughly broken.

But when they pass the handkerchief back to you, and you shake it open, the match falls out intact and unharmed.

And it has the identifying crayon mark on it to show it's the same as the one before!

THE SECRET: Before you start, slide the spare match into the hem of the handkerchief. Tuck it well down so that it is completely out of sight.

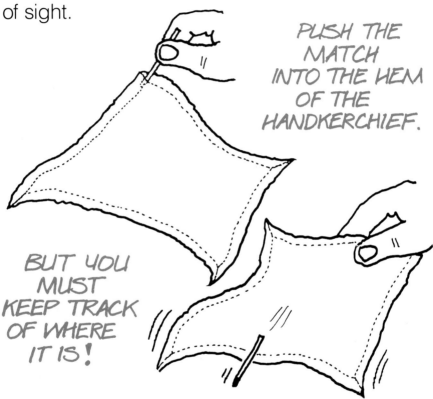

PUSH THE MATCH INTO THE HEM OF THE HANDKERCHIEF.

BUT YOU MUST KEEP TRACK OF WHERE IT IS!

Then make sure, when you fold the handkerchief, that you keep track of that particular part of the hem. That's where you want the member of the audience to feel for the match. And THAT'S the match that is broken, not the other one!

The magic cereal box

You will need:

two small empty cereal boxes with liner bags
  (they must be identical)

glue

scissors

double-sided sticky tape

a plastic knife

a dish towel

This is a neat illusion that makes a good opener for your magic act.

First, you show the audience an empty box of cereal. Then you fling a dish towel over it, wave your wand, and the box is magically filled to the brim with cornflakes.

THE SECRET: The box has a hidden compartment at the bottom filled with cornflakes. Also, the design and wording on the back of the box are the wrong way up. This means that the box is reversible and you can flip it over without anyone realizing that you have turned it upside down. In fact, you turn over the box (as our drawing shows) while draping the dish towel over it. Clever stuff!

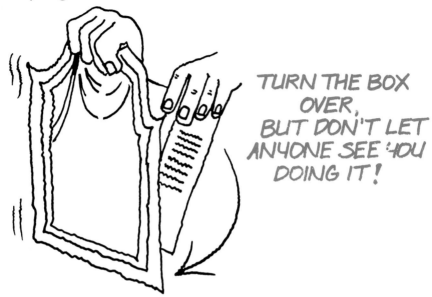

TURN THE BOX
OVER,
BUT DON'T LET
ANYONE SEE YOU
DOING IT!

PREPARATION: Pry up the top and bottom flaps of the two boxes very carefully with a plastic knife. Then cut the front design and top flaps from one box and glue them to the back and bottom of the other one, making sure that they are upside down (our drawing shows how the outside of the box should look.) Then cut the two lining bags. One should be about three-quarters of its original length. The other needs to be trimmed down until it is only a quarter of its right size. When you've got them the correct length, glue them end to end and slide them into the box. Fill the small compartment with cornflakes and lightly seal the flaps with small squares of double-sided sticky tape. Do the same with the flaps at the other end, and your trick cereal box is complete!

TAKE THE FRONT FROM ONE CEREAL BOX...

...AND GLUE IT TO THE BACK OF THE OTHER ONE UPSIDE DOWN

corn flakes

FIRST LINING BAG

SECOND LINING BAG

GLUE THEM TOGETHER

The great newspaper carve-up

You will need:

a sheet of newspaper

a tube of rubber cement

scissors

Have you ever watched a magician cut up a strip of newspaper and then stared in disbelief as the paper magically joined itself together again?

It's a super trick that never fails to impress but, amazingly, it requires no special magic skills whatsoever! The secret lies in the crafty way the paper is prepared beforehand.

First, fold the sheet in half as our drawing shows. Then flatten it out and smear a coat of rubber cement three inches (7cm) on either side of the fold mark.

When the coating is dry, go over it with a second application of cement and leave it to dry. When you've done that, give it a third coat. Wait until it is completely dry again and then dust the coated area with flour to cover up any faint discoloration caused by the cement. Your "magic" newspaper is now ready for use.

TAKE A SHEET OF NEWSPAPER AND FOLD IT IN HALF...

... SPREAD GLUE ON EITHER SIDE OF THE FOLD MARK...

Cut a two inch (5cm) strip off the paper from top to bottom, look for the fold in the middle, and crease it again in that place. Now snip the paper through the cement area at the fold mark with scissors as our picture shows.

By rights, you should now have two lengths of paper in your hand but when the strips are shaken out and held up, the two ends magically bind together. They are gripped, of course, by all that rubber cement but your audience will put it down to your amazing magical powers!

...CUT A STRIP FROM ONE END OF THE PAPER...

...FOLD THE STRIP AND CUT THROUGH THE CEMENT AREA...

THE TWO ENDS BIND TOGETHER — HELD BY THE CEMENT!

Magic with special apparatus

The double-sided envelope

You will need:

two identical envelopes

glue

This is a trick device, something that magicians call a "piece of apparatus," that you can use in lots of ways.

It's made by glueing the address sides of two envelopes together as our drawing shows, making sure that no edges overlap.

If you do the job carefully, you will have what appears to be a perfectly ordinary envelope when viewed by the audience (as long as they see only one side of it!). In fact, of course, ANOTHER envelope with ANOTHER compartment will be glued to the back.

This means that if you place, say, a playing card in the front compartment, then secretly reverse the envelope and open the back compartment, the playing card will have magically disappeared!

TAKE TWO
IDENTICAL
ENVELOPES...

AND GLUE THEM
TOGETHER,
FRONT TO FRONT.

Double-sided envelopes can be used to
make writing disappear on blank paper, turn one
playing card into another, change blue stamps
into red ones, and make dozens of things
disappear and reappear at your command!
  Now read on...

Crying baby

You will need:

a double-sided envelope

plain white cardboard

tracing paper

a pencil and ballpoint pen

a letter opener

For this trick you will need two plain white pieces of cardboard the same shape and size as a playing card. Trace the picture of the crying baby on one, and the picture of the sleeping baby on the other. Then go over the outlines with a ballpoint pen so that both the drawings are clear.

HIDE THE
"SLEEPING BABY"
IN THE
ENVELOPE...

Finally, seal up the picture of the sleeping baby in the secret compartment of your double-sided envelope, and tell this story...

45

"Our baby (hold up the card with the crying baby on it) was howling his head off yesterday, and I couldn't do a thing with him.

"I tried picking him up (hold the card in two hands as if you were picking up a real baby) and THAT didn't work.

"I tried patting his back (turn the card over and tap your fingers on the blank side) and THAT didn't work. I tried playing with him (jiggle the card between your hands) and THAT didn't work.

... PUT THE "CRYING BABY" TO BED.

"And then I thought, 'Perhaps he's tired and wants to go to bed.' So I took him up to his crib (pick up the double-sided envelope) and made sure it was all comfy for him (open the envelope to show that it is empty) and I put him down and tucked him in (put the card in the envelope and seal it up) and hoped for the best.

"I rocked the crib for a while (wave the envelope to and fro) and he STOPPED crying!

46

"Then his eyes started to close, and, very quietly, I slipped away. (Put the envelope down on a table, reversing it at the same time, and then tip-toe away from it.)

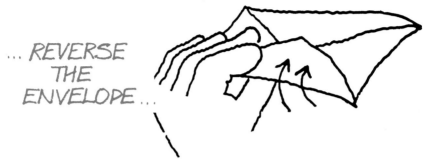

... *REVERSE THE ENVELOPE*...

"And guess what? There wasn't another peep out of him all morning. And when I looked in later (slit open the envelope and hold up the picture of the sleeping baby) he was STILL fast asleep! Now isn't that amazing?"

...*" AND HE WAS STILL FAST ASLEEP!"*

DON'T use a kitchen knife or pointed scissors to slit open your envelope. You can buy a safe letter opener at fairly low cost in most stores that sell stationery. A narrow ruler or plastic picnic knife would also work.

Getting over the chicken pox

You will need:

a double-sided envelope

plain white cardboard

tracing paper

a pencil

two ballpoint pens (one red, one black)

a safety pin

a letter opener

This is a similar routine to the Crying Baby and works in much the same way. Start by tracing the face on each of the two identical pieces of cardboard. Go over the outlines with a black ballpoint pen and then put lots of red spots on one of the faces. Seal the OTHER card (without the spots) in the secret compartment of your double-sided envelope, and you're ready to begin.

This is the story:

"When my friend John caught chicken pox he looked REALLY horrible! He was covered with red spots.

"Well, as you can imagine, he was put straight to bed (pop the card in the envelope and seal it up), and everybody had to stay away from him. (Put the card on the table, reversing it at the same time, and walk away.)

"After a little while the doctor came and gave John this shot (now plunge the safety pin straight through the envelope), which John hated. I wouldn't like that very much either, would you? But it seemed to work because when I went to see him a couple of days later (remove the safety pin and slit open the envelope), all his spots had GONE (hold up the card). And now he's perfectly all right!"

Sawing a lady in half

You will need:

a double-sided envelope

a queen from two identical decks of playing cards

scissors

a letter opener

You can have lots of fun with this trick!

Sawing a lady in half is probably the most famous magical illusion in the world, and YOU are about to perform it. Wow!

Unfortunately, one or two problems cropped up in rehearsals, you tell the audience.

As a result, your sister, who was helping you, is now in the hospital—wards 1 and 2. (Don't scream, Mom it's only a joke!)

Also, the man next door came and took his saw back.

Certain minor changes have had to be made in the act, therefore.

The lady and the saw have been dropped. (They were just a nuisance anyway.)

Instead, you will be cutting up a picture of a lady with a pair of scissors.

This is in many ways much more DIFFICULT AND DANGEROUS than the other version, because you will be cutting up a playing card, from the deck your Dad plays Bridge with, and he won't be pleased if you can't get it back together again.

But, of course, the card is restored perfectly after the pieces have been sealed up in an envelope (the double-sided one) which has special powers.

Great fun!

STEP 1.

STEP 2.

STEP 3.

Squaring the circle

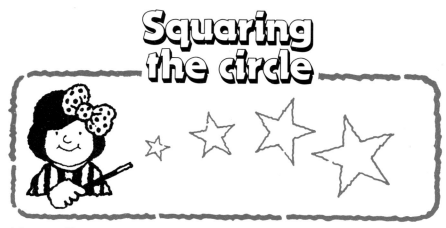

You will need:

a double-sided envelope

plain white cardboard

a black crayon or felt-tip pen

a letter opener

Squaring the Circle is another famous stage illusion that has baffled audiences for years. The magician twirls a steel hoop between his fingers and suddenly, in front of everyone's eyes, it turns into a square frame.

It's a trick that takes practice and dexterity, not to mention some very special metal work, so this is NOT the version you are going to perform!

For your illusion a trusty double-sided envelope plus two cards, one with a circle drawn on it, and one with a square, will do just as well! Follow a similar routine to Crying Baby or Sawing a Lady in Half and the audience will love it. Well, hopefully!

The Emperor's new clothes

You will need:

a double-sided envelope

three squares of white cardboard

tracing paper

a pencil

your paintbox

a letter opener

Do you remember the famous story by Hans Christian Andersen about the emperor who ordered some new clothes? He was told that the material they would be made from was so fine that it could only be seen by very intelligent people. To everyone else his clothes would be invisible.

The emperor, who was obviously the biggest fool of his day, fell for this piece of hokum, with disastrous results.

With the help of the double-sided envelope, YOU can now reveal what happened on the day he wore the clothes (or THOUGHT he was wearing them!).

To prepare, trace each drawing of the emperor on a square of white cardboard, then use your paints to color the pictures as neatly as possible. Do the same with the drawing of the two cheating tailors.

When everything is ready, seal up the picture of the naked emperor in the secret compartment of the double-sided envelope. Put it in back to front so that when it is taken out, the blank side of the card will be facing the audience.

As you start the story, show the audience the pictures of the (clothed) emperor and the tailors.

Then say: "The tailors promised to have the new clothes ready on the day of the royal procession through the city. The emperor could hardly wait.

"When the day dawned, he dashed into the royal chambers, cleared everybody out, made sure he was completely alone (show the envelope to be empty), and invited the tailors in." (Pop the picture of the tailors into the envelope.)

"Then he looked around to make sure no one was watching (show the emperor's picture to the audience at different angles) and slipped in behind them." (Now turn the picture around so that the blank side is toward the audience, then place it in the envelope.)

"And finally, of course, he locked the door." (Seal the envelope and put it down on a table, reversing it at the same time.)

"The tailors helped the emperor into his new clothes, said he looked smashing, and vanished. No one ever saw them again. And when the emperor came out of the dressing room (slit open the envelope and take out the card, keeping the blank side to the audience) everybody said, 'Oh, you look SUPER in that outfit,' because of course, nobody wanted to be thought of as a dum-dum—and, remember, you could only see these clothes if you were very intelligent.

"And all along the route of the procession people said, 'Doesn't he look great in his new clothes?' all pretending to each other that they could see them.

"Except for ONE little boy who shouted out, 'He hasn't got any clothes on!' and started to laugh.

"And then EVERYBODY started to laugh, because that little boy (slowly turn the card around so that the picture of the naked emperor comes into the audience's view) was absolutely RIGHT!

"Or could it just be that none of us here is intelligent enough to see the new clothes? Hands up everybody who can see them. (Pause) What! No one? Well, well, well!"

The tapered deck

You will need:

a deck of playing cards

scissors

The tapered deck looks like a perfectly ordinary deck of playing cards, but it isn't. Each card is slightly trimmed so that one end is narrower than the other. This tapering is so fine that it's almost impossible to detect when the narrow ends are all together. But the moment a card is pulled out and inserted in the deck THE OTHER WAY AROUND, the overlapping edge is easy to feel. More important, you can actually pull the card straight out.

As you can imagine, this secret advantage can be put to use in a variety of ways in a magic show.

You can make up your own tapered deck by trimming the cards carefully one at a time with a pair of scissors, using the first card you cut as a guide for the others.

But, of course, it would be better to do the job with a paper cutter—a type of equipment which a printing shop, photo lab, or art studio is likely to have. If you know people who work in such a place, try and get them to do it for you.

If that fails and you don't want to try cutting the cards yourself, you'll find that most shops that sell tricks have decks of "magic cards" that you can buy, usually at fairly low cost.

Now let's see some of the clever things you can do with the deck...

Mind reading

You will need:

a tapered deck

Hold the deck face down and fan the cards. Then ask a member of the audience to take one. It can be any card they please.

ASK A MEMBER OF THE AUDIENCE TO "PICK A CARD"

Tell him to look at it without showing you. While he is doing this, tidy the cards in your hands and TURN THE DECK AROUND. Then fan the cards again and tell him to slide the card back in the deck anywhere he chooses. Make sure he doesn't accidentally turn the card

TURN
THE DECK
AROUND...

...AND ASK THE
PERSON TO
REPLACE THE CARD

around when he does this. (If that should happen, you will have to gather up the cards, reverse the deck, and make a new fan.)

Now hold the deck behind your back and tell the person in the audience to concentrate hard on the card he chose.

At the same time, feel for the wrong-way-around card and carefully pull it out. After you think the person has "concentrated" for long enough, produce the card from behind your back and watch to see the look on his face!

The heavy kings

You will need:

a tapered deck

Before you start, take the four kings from the deck and replace them in different places and the wrong way around. When you've done that, you're ready to begin.

TAKE OUT
ALL THE KINGS
BEFORE YOU START.

Start by handing the deck to a member of the audience. Ask her to look through the cards to make sure the four kings are there.

Then shuffle the deck, making sure you don't drop any, and explain that the four kings (and not many people know this!) have more detail on them and are printed over a larger area than any of the other cards and this of course, makes them heavier than the rest!

FEEL FOR THE CARDS.

YOU CAN FIND THE FOUR KINGS WHEN YOU HOLD THE DECK BEHIND YOUR BACK.

In fact, you always know where these particular cards are in the deck because they weigh so much! Take the deck behind your back and pull out the four turned around cards. Then pretend to struggle with a heavy weight four times, and produce them for the audience to see.

Finally, pass the rest of the cards back to the member of the audience so that she can see that the four kings REALLY WERE out of the deck, and not from your back pocket!

The amazing choice

You will need:

a tapered deck

This trick requires no special preparation. Ask a member of the audience to choose any card from the deck and look at it without showing you. Then turn the tapered deck around, and get him to replace the card somewhere in the middle. The broad edge of the chosen card will now be at the narrow end of the deck, and easy for you to find.

LIFT OFF A BUNDLE OF CARDS TO "CUT" THE DECK...

Now comes the fun! Shuffle the cards and put the deck face up on the table. Now get ready to cut the deck. Feel down the pile until you find the broad-edged card, and cut the deck in that place. When the cards are put back together, the chosen card will then be at the BOTTOM of the pile.

Now pick up the deck, turn it over in your hand (so that the cards are face down), and deal out two rows of six cards each, all face down. The chosen card, of course, will be the first one dealt, but you are the only person to know this!

THE CHOSEN CARD IS THE FIRST ONE DEALT!

Now ask the member of the audience to choose one of the two rows of cards. But don't tell him why! If he chooses the row WITHOUT the special card in it, gather up those six cards and put them back with the rest of the deck. If he chooses the row WITH the special card in it, then put the other row away on the wastepile, as it is clearly unwanted!

Next, divide the six cards on the table into two groups of three, and ask the person to choose again. As before, make sure you discard the group WITHOUT the chosen card in it.

Now you are down to just three cards. Ask him to choose two of the three cards. If the special card is not one of the ones chosen, you are home free! Discard the chosen pair and the remaining card is the very one pulled out from the deck in the first place.

But if the special card is one of the two he pointed to, you still have some work to do. Slide the chosen pair to the front of the table, discard the (non chosen) third card and ask him to choose again.

If he selects the WRONG one, ask him if he is absolutely sure! When he says he is, pick up the rest of the deck, place the wrong card carefully into the middle of it, pass the deck across to him, and ask him to look for the card he originally chose.

Of course, it won't be there. It is the one card still left on the table. So pick it up with a flourish and wait for the applause!

Needless to say, you won't need to bother with this final maneuver if he chooses the CORRECT card out of the last pair. Just let him pick it up and confirm that it's the right one. Clever you!

The magic box

You will need:

a wooden cigar box

cardboard

scissors

a paintbrush

non-glossy black paint

varnish

The magic box is an essential piece of apparatus for every young magician.

With it you can make cards and small objects appear and disappear at will, or alter their shape, size, and color.

You can buy a magic box ready-made at shops that supply magic equipment. But it's more fun to make one yourself if you can.

The kind of cigar box you'll need must have a hinged lid, and the lid must be deep enough to house a secret compartment!

You'll want enough room there to hide various small objects like buttons and badges or a key or a playing card.

When the lid is up, these secret items will be out of sight behind a loose flap of cardboard painted the same color (non-glossy black) as the rest of the inside of the box. To the audience

HIDE OBJECTS BEHIND THE FLAP OF BLACK CARD...

...CLOSE THE LID AND SAY THE MAGIC SPELL...

...HEY PRESTO! THE FLAP FALLS DOWN TO REVEAL THE HIDDEN OBJECTS.

the flap appears to be simply the inside of the lid. But, of course, it's nothing of the kind!

As soon as the lid is closed, the flap falls to the floor of the box, bringing down everything you've hidden in the secret compartment and covering up whatever was put in the bottom of the box a moment before!

As you can imagine, the number of tricks you can perform with a clever piece of apparatus like this is almost endless.

The secret of making a successful magic box is in the painting. The color black is one of the most useful aids a magician can call upon because it is so very hard to see. So if you make sure the inside of the box, plus the sides and edges of the flap, are liberally coated in non-glossy black, you will have a first-class trick box that you can use in a variety of ways even in close up magic situations.

A final word about the outside of the box. You should remove the maker's labels and then give all the surfaces two or three coats of thick varnish to make them as shiny as possible. You want them to "glare," because this makes it even harder for the audience to adjust their eyes and spot the secret flap in the inky black interior of the box.

Now let's look at some of the tricks you can perform with your magic box...

Card predictions

You will need:

a deck of playing cards

an envelope

a sheet of paper

a ballpoint pen

a magic box

Before you begin, take any card from the deck (say the five of hearts) and hide it in the secret compartment of your magic box.

MAKE SURE THAT YOU PUT THE CARD IN THE RIGHT WAY AROUND.

At the end of the trick it must appear in the box FACE DOWN, so make sure you put it in the compartment the right way around.

Then write FIVE OF HEARTS on a sheet of paper and seal it in an envelope. When you've done this, you're ready to present the trick.

Start by saying that you have a perfectly ordinary deck of cards, not a trick deck, and you would like a member of the audience to examine it (one card will be missing, of course, but that won't be noticed).

Ask him to pay particular attention to the faces of the cards to make sure they are all different.

When he is satisfied that the deck is genuine, spread the cards face down on the table and ask someone else in the audience to put a finger on one of them.

When the choice is made, ask her if she knows what card her finger is on. She will answer no, of course, because all the cards are face down.

Now tell everyone that there is no way YOU could know what card it is either—and to make sure the choice stays COMPLETELY UNKNOWN to you and everybody else present, you want her to place the card face down in this empty box (your magic box) close the lid, and hold the box on her lap.

Now produce the sealed envelope and ask another person in the audience to open it and read out what's written on the paper inside.

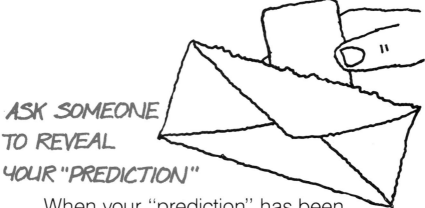

ASK SOMEONE TO REVEAL YOUR "PREDICTION"

When your "prediction" has been announced, get your magic box back from the person who has been holding it, move a step or two back from the audience "so that everyone can see" (in fact, you don't want them to spot the flap!), raise the lid and take out the card. Don't look at it—simply hold it up to the audience and say, "Tell me what it is".

And, of course, your "prediction" will have proved absolutely correct!

The chocolate box

You will need:

a box of chocolate cookies

the label from the box (cut it out before you begin)

a strip of transparent tape

a magic box

This is a simple but effective trick to perform at a party for young children.

Hold up your magic box to show there is nothing in it, then close the lid and put the box down on the table.

Now take the label from the chocolate cookie box and tape it to the front of the magic box.

Hold up the box so that everyone can see the label, tap it with your wand, and then raise the lid.

To everyone's surprise and delight, the box is now loaded with chocolate cookies. Pass them around for the audience to enjoy.

THE SECRET: the chocolate cookies are stored in the secret compartment of your magic box, of course. The number you can pack in there will depend on the size of your box. If there's space for two rows, so much the better!

The bull and the tramp

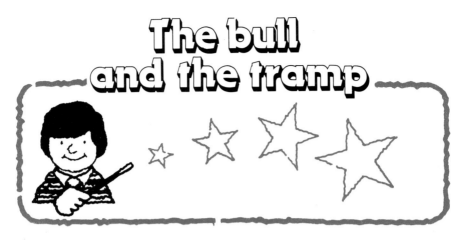

You will need:

four squares of white construction paper, each about the size of a playing card

a slightly larger square of yellow construction paper

a strip of bright red material or cloth

tracing paper

a pencil

paper clips

your paintbox

scissors

glue

a magic box

This trick will take you a little time to prepare, but you'll find the effort very worthwhile.

Start by tracing the picture of the tramp onto one of the squares of white construction paper. Now trace it again onto one of the other squares. Try to position the two drawings in the same place on each square.

76

Now repeat the process with the bull, tracing the picture on two squares of white construction paper in the same way.

Then trace the sheaf of wheat FOUR TIMES on the yellow construction paper (don't worry about the positioning, because they will be cut up later).

Finally, trace the tramp's trousers and then cut out the tracing to use as a paper pattern.

VERY CAREFULLY CUT AROUND THE PAPER PATTERN.

You will need enough red material to make up two pairs of trousers. Clip the tracing to the cloth as firmly as you can, then cut around the outline. Do the same again for the second pair.

When that's done, you can start coloring the drawings. The two pictures of the tramp must be identical, so use exactly the same colors on each. The same goes for the two pictures of the bull.

When you come to perform the trick, the audience must believe there is only one drawing not two. That's why it's very important to match the colors and brush strokes on the two pictures as closely as possible.

The sheaves of wheat will need painting, too. Try to make them as realistic as possible, and then cut out each one as neatly as you can.

Now for the tramp's trousers. Glue them in place on him in just one of the drawings. On the SECOND drawing glue a sheaf of wheat there instead!

Finally, stick the second pair of trousers around the bull's horns on one of the two bull drawings.

When everything is ready, hide three of the drawings, the bull with the trousers on its horns, the tramp wearing a sheaf of wheat, and one of the other sheaves, in the secret compartment of your magic box.

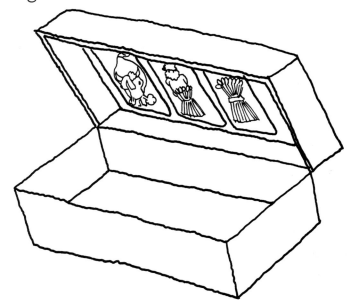

The trick you are going to perform is not so much an act of magic as a piece of entertaining fiction, so you will need to present it with a twinkle in your eye!

This is the story you tell:

Tom the tramp was out walking one day in the countryside. It was a very hot day, and Tom soon began to feel tired.

"Now where can I find a nice soft bed to fall asleep on?," he wondered.

Just then he spotted exactly what he was looking for. In the next field was a barn with lots of lovely soft bundles of hay to lie on!

Well, you can imagine, Tom was delighted. He skipped over the hedge and set off across the field as fast as his tired legs could carry him.

Now in the corner of the field, quietly munching away, was Angus the bull.

Of course, sleepy Tom hadn't noticed Angus there.

But Angus noticed HIM. He took one look at Tom's bright red trousers and began to charge!

Tom ran into the barn, and Angus chased straight after him. What a rumpus there was!

And when Angus finally came out, as you can see, Tom wasn't wearing his bright red trousers anymore. Angus had them on his horns!

Now what was poor Tom going to do without his trousers? Oh, dear!

He had to wear a sheaf of wheat until he could afford to buy another pair!

Great fun! And I'm sure you can work out the right moments in the story to pop the various pictures in the magic box (which is, of course, the "barn") without my needing to tell you !

The magic of numbers

The magic of numbers

Think of a number. Double it. Add five. Add twelve. Take away three. Halve it. Now take away the number you first thought of.

THE ANSWER IS SEVEN.

Magic? It certainly looks that way, but in fact it's simple arithmetic! And it never fails so long as the person doing the sums gets them right!

Number tricks have been around forever, but they're probably more popular now than ever before. So it's well worth including one or two in any magic show you put on.

Here's a selection to choose from. You'll find it's best to provide the person doing the sums with a pencil and paper (or a calculator for big-figure tricks).

Two's company

Here's a simple number trick you can perform with a very young audience.

1. Think of a number between one and ten.
2. Double it.
3. Add four.
4. Divide by two.
5. Take away the number you first thought of.
6. The answer is TWO!

IF THE NUMBER IS THREE :

DOUBLE IT = 6
ADD FOUR = 10
DIVIDE BY TWO = 5
TAKE AWAY THREE = 2 !

THE SECRET: The answer will always be half of the number you select to be added in Step 3. Had you said, "Add six," the answer would have been THREE—and so on.

As you were

You will need to give the person doing this sum a pencil and paper unless his mental arithmetic is very good.

1. Think of a number (say 3).

2. Multiply it by three (9).

3. Add two (11).

4. Multiply by three again (33).

5. Add the number you first thought of (36).

6. Add two (38).

7. Make the last number a zero (30).

8. Divide by ten (3).

9. And that's the number you first thought of!

NOTE: You can do this trick with numbers greater than ten!

Freaky family

This is a trick for people with big families! Before you begin, get the person doing the sum to count up all the aunts, uncles and cousins he or she has. Then:

1. Add the number of aunts and uncles together (say 4 + 5 = 9).

2. Double it (18).

3. Add three (21).

4. Multiply by five (105).

5. Now add all the cousins—say six (111).

6. Take away 15 (96).

Now see the two figures you've arrived at. The one on the left is the number of aunts and uncles, and on the right is the number of cousins.

The amazing number nine

Nine is a very mysterious number. Lots of tricks you can do with numbers end up with nine as the answer.

For instance, if you add together all the digits from one to nine (1 + 2 + 3 + 4 + 5 + 6 + 7 + 8 + 9) you get 45. And if you add four and five together you get nine.

Now take away all the digits (123456789) from the same lot in reverse order (987654321) the answer is 846,197,532. Add those digits together (8 + 4 + 6 + 1 + 9 + 7 + 5 + 3 + 2) and the answer is 45 again. And we know what four and five add up to, don't we?

Here's another oddity: choose any large number—say 687,481—and multiply it by nine. The answer in this case is 6,187,329. Now add the digits together (6 + 1 + 8 + 7 + 3 + 2 + 9) and the answer is 36. Add three and six and the answer is, yes, NINE again!

You can put the power of the number nine to good use in your magic show. Before you begin, write NINE on a piece of paper, seal it in an envelope and give it to a member of the audience to hold. Then ask him to:

1. Write down any four numbers from one to nine (say 7914).
2. Add the digits together (7 + 9 + 1 + 4 = 21).
3. Take away the sum from the original number (7914 - 21 = 7893).
4. Add the digits together (7 + 8 + 9 + 3 = 27).
5. Add those digits (2 + 7 = 9).

And THAT'S the number you sealed in the envelope!

The amazing number nine again

Here's another baffler involving that freaky number nine.

1. Ask anyone in the audience to call out a seven figure phone number: let's say it's 987—8236.

2. Ask another member of the audience to JUMBLE UP the digits. Let's say you get 762—8839.

3. Now take away the smaller number from the larger one (9878236—7628839 = 2249397).

4. Add the digits together
   (2 + 2 + 4 + 9 + 3 + 9 + 7 = 36).

5. Now add three and six together and the answer is NINE.

The amazing number nine yet again

If you're still not convinced about the strange power of number nine, try this on your calculator.

1. Tap in all the digits except eight (12345679).
2. Choose any one digit from the list (say 3).
3. Multiply it by NINE = 27.
4. Now multiply that number by the string of digits you first wrote down:
   27 x 12345679.
5. The answer is 333,333,333, the number you chose repeated NINE times over!

You will get the same amazing result, a row of identical figures, no matter which number you choose from the list. Why? It's that weird number nine up to its tricks again!

The mind boggler

Here's a number trick that seems quite impossible. But beware—it will go wrong if the person who does the sums isn't very good at math! So make sure he or she has a pencil and paper or, preferably, a calculator to work with.

1. Take your age (13) say.
2. Double it (26).
3. Add five (31).
4. Multiply by 50 (1550).
5. Add the amount of LOOSE CHANGE under $1.00 in your pocket or purse, say 31 cents (1581).
6. Take away the number of DAYS IN THE YEAR (1581 - 365 = 1216).
7. Add 115 (1331).
8. Divide by 100 (13.31).

Now see where the decimal point comes. Your age will be to the LEFT and your loose change to the RIGHT. Fantastic!

Odd nineteen

Like the Mind Boggler, this is one of the most baffling number tricks ever devised. Before you begin, write the number NINETEEN on a piece of paper, then fold it up and seal it in an envelope. Give the envelope to a member of the audience to look after. Then ask him to:

1. Think of a number greater than one (say 39).
2. Add five (44).
3. Multiply by three (132).
4. Take away one (131).
5. Add the digits together (1 + 3 + 1 = 5).
6. Multiply by three (15).
7. Add two (17).
8. Add the digits together (1 + 7 = 8).
9. Double it (16).
10. Add three (19).

And THAT is the number sealed up in the envelope. At least it should be. If it isn't, the person in the audience must have chosen 995 to start with. That's the only number that DOESN'T come out to 19. Odd!

This is a trick with dominoes, or rather, the numbers on a domino. Before you begin, put all the dominoes in a bag and give them a good shake. Then invite a friend in the audience to feel inside the bag and take out a single domino without showing you what it is. Then tell your friend to:

1. Multiply the HIGHEST number by five.
2. Add seven to it.
3. Double it.
4. Add the LOWEST number on the domino.
5. Take away 14.

Now ask for the answer. Suppose it's 42. The two figures that make up the answer, four and two, are the same two numbers on the domino. Impossible? Try it for yourself and see!

How old are you?

Here's another way of having fun with figures. Look down the six columns and find which ones contain your age. Then add together the figures at the TOP of those particular columns and that's how old you are!

1	2	4	8	16	32
3	3	5	9	17	33
5	6	6	10	18	34
7	7	7	11	19	35
9	10	12	12	20	36
11	11	13	13	21	37
13	14	14	14	22	38
15	15	15	15	23	39
17	18	20	24	24	40
19	19	21	25	25	41
21	22	22	26	26	42
23	23	23	27	27	43
25	26	28	28	28	44
27	27	29	29	29	45
29	30	30	30	30	46
31	31	31	31	31	47
33	34	36	40	48	48
35	35	37	41	49	49
37	38	38	42	50	50
39	39	39	43	51	51
41	42	44	44	52	52
43	43	45	45	53	53
45	46	46	46	54	54
47	47	47	47	55	55
49	50	52	56	56	56
51	51	53	57	57	57
53	54	54	58	58	58
55	55	55	59	59	59
57	58	60	60	60	60
59	59	61	61	61	61
61	62	62	62	62	62
63	63	63	63	63	63